All Things Self Care

BOOK STORE

Books for The Soul

Oops, I Joined a Cult & Didn't Know It

The Business of Religion

By: Speaking Freedom Books

Concept By: Dr. Kaci (Winslow) Myers

ISBN: 978-1-944901-52-3

Copyright © 2025 by Speaking Freedom LLC
All rights reserved.
No portion of this book may be reproduced without written permission from the publisher or author, except as permitted by U.S. copyright law.

Book Cover by: Kaci Winslow

Publisher Website: speakingfreedom.org

Other Website Information:
SpeakingfreedomTV.org, edu-freedom.org

Publisher Address: 75 Washington St. #1177, Fairburn, GA 30213

Introduction: When Faith Meets the Fine Print

I didn't join a cult. At least, that's what I thought.

When I left the Army and moved to Atlanta, I was looking for a sense of belonging, peace, purpose, and community. The church I found offered all of that and more. The music was alive, the sermons were moving, and the people were warm. I joined as a member, served as an usher, and eventually worked behind the scenes in administration.

That's when things changed.

Once I stepped into the back offices, I saw another side of the ministry that looked less like a sanctuary and more like a corporation. I watched budgets prioritized over people, competition hidden behind smiles, and strategic marketing plans disguised as "outreach." I saw leadership fights that would make political campaigns blush, and spiritual manipulation used to silence anyone who asked questions.

At first, I excused it all. I told myself these were "attacks of the enemy." I thought the criticism and online blogs exposing churches like ours were persecution, not accountability.

Then one day, I stumbled across a website, *rickross.com*, where a list titled **"10 Warning Signs of a Cult"** stopped me cold. One by one, I read traits that sounded eerily familiar: unquestioned authority, isolation from dissent, financial manipulation, and fear-based loyalty. I remember sitting there, heart racing, realizing that what I'd given my devotion to might have been built on more than just faith; it was built on a formula.

That was my awakening.

It wasn't a loss of faith but a rebirth of discernment.

As I matured, I began studying psychology, history, and spirituality. I learned how belief systems shape the brain, how trauma seeks belonging, and how religion evolved as both a moral guide and a social control system. The deeper I studied, the clearer it became that I hadn't left God; I had simply outgrown the business of religion.

The more I separated systems from Spirit, the closer I grew to God's *omni divine presence*, the Source that exists beyond pulpits, politics, and profit margins.

Chapter 1: When Worship Becomes Industry

Faith didn't start as a business. It began as belonging.

Before temples, churches, or offerings, people sought connection with nature, the unseen, and one another. They expressed reverence through what they had: the harvest, the animals, their labor, and their songs. These early acts of giving were not payments; they were gratitude in motion. The intent was simple to acknowledge something greater and share that awareness with the community.

As people gathered more consistently, patterns formed. Someone began organizing the rituals. Someone else managed supplies, and soon, structure was born. Order made faith easier to share, but it also made it possible to manage, and anything that can be managed can eventually be monetized. What began as a service gradually turned into a system.

In time, those responsible for maintaining the system became authorities within it. Temples needed caretakers, and sacred spaces required resources. Leaders were appointed to keep things balanced, but balance is difficult to sustain when survival depends on contribution. Slowly, *offerings turned into obligations.* People began to give not only out of gratitude but also out of expectation, hoping their gift would guarantee favor, healing, or security.

That was the earliest form of religious transaction. Not manipulation evolution. A structure trying to sustain itself began teaching that blessing and obedience were connected. The heart of worship remained, but the message shifted from "give because you love" to "love is proven by what you give."

Centuries later, this framework matured into what we now recognize as the business of religion. It's not just about money; it's about maintenance. Faith communities run on the same practical needs as any organization: resources, leadership, planning, and communication. The difference is that spiritual systems often claim divine authority, which makes accountability harder to apply. When leaders equate disagreement with disobedience, a culture of compliance quietly replaces a culture of curiosity.

Still, most leaders don't intend harm. They're often following inherited models that worked for generations before them. What they teach is what they were taught that stability is sacred, and order is proof of excellence. Few realize that the structure can become a subtle form of control when the focus shifts from nurturing people to preserving programs.

The Industrial Age of Religion only expanded this pattern. Printing presses allowed theology to spread like a product. Television and radio turned preachers into personalities. Now, digital media has made ministries global and faith entirely online. None of this is inherently negative; it has given millions access to wisdom and hope, but it has also turned belief into an algorithm.

Today, worship competes with entertainment. Influence often determines credibility more than integrity does. It's common to see celebrities or online figures publicly turn toward faith, quoting scripture as part of a brand narrative. Many are sincere, but the pattern reflects something deeper: religion remains one of the most powerful marketing tools ever created. It sells belonging, redemption, and reassurance, which everyone desires.

This is where faith begins to resemble a subscription model. You give, it works; you stop, it doesn't. Attendance and contribution become proof of alignment. The formula is familiar because it mirrors every other service-based system in society. The difference is that spiritual subscription plays on eternal stakes, loss of favor, blessing, or salvation. The message becomes, "Stay connected or risk disconnecting from God."

That's not an accusation; it's an observation. It explains why so many sincere believers feel guilty when questioning institutions or stepping away from them. The system isn't built to release; it's built to retain. Loyalty becomes codependency, and dependency becomes identity. Once that happens, discernment fades, replaced by routine.

Understanding this evolution helps restore balance. Religion isn't the enemy. It's a vessel that can carry truth or tradition depending on who's steering it. The goal isn't to destroy structure, but to remember that structure was meant to serve Spirit, not contain it.

As we move forward, we'll look more closely at how these systems reinforce themselves: how authority, belonging, and fear interlock to keep faith functional but sometimes unfree. To truly understand the business of religion, we must first understand the architecture that sustains it.

As the book unfolds, we'll explore how psychology, trauma, and culture all contribute to this dynamic and how to tell the difference between *spiritual alignment* and *spiritual entrapment*.

Chapter 2: The Architecture of Control

Every system has a structure. Without structure, there's chaos. However, once a structure exists, someone has to manage it, and that is where control begins to take shape.

Religion is no different. What starts as shared faith soon develops levels of responsibility: teachers, caretakers, leaders, and followers. Each role serves a purpose, yet the more defined the hierarchy becomes, the easier it is for guidance to turn into governance. The transition is rarely intentional. It happens quietly, through repetition and trust.

The Need for Order

Faith communities thrive on predictability. Regular meetings, known leaders, and familiar rituals create safety. Humans crave stability, especially in matters of the spirit. Structure answers that are needed by providing clear expectations: what to believe, how to behave, when to gather, and how to give. Over time, these expectations become traditions, and traditions begin to feel sacred simply because they're familiar.

Order, by itself, isn't the problem. The challenge comes when order is mistaken for holiness. When a process that once served as a connection becomes the *proof* of connection, control has already entered the conversation.

Authority and Obedience

Leadership is necessary; absolute authority is not. Healthy spiritual guidance points people back to their own connection with the Divine. Unhealthy authority redirects that connection toward the leader. The shift is subtle: sermons begin to include phrases like "stay under covering," "don't question what God is doing," or "touch not my anointed." These messages sound protective, but often train believers to equate disagreement with disobedience.

When questioning is discouraged, discernment atrophies. People learn to obey before understanding, and obedience without understanding becomes dependent. That dependence sustains control, not through fear alone but through emotional loyalty.

Belonging and Behavior

Humans are social by design. We seek belonging even more than we seek truth. In a faith setting, community becomes identity. Language, dress, and shared values signal who is "in" and "out." This sense of belonging is powerful; it can heal loneliness and offer purpose. But it can also bind people to conformity. When inclusion depends on agreement, individuality feels like rebellion.

The psychology behind this is simple: we fear exclusion. Losing our group can feel like losing God, so we stay even when the structure stops serving growth. That emotional equation, belonging = righteousness, keeps people anchored long after their beliefs have shifted.

Fear as Foundation

Every enduring system uses motivation. Some use inspiration, others use fear. Religious control often mixes both. The promise of blessing motivates giving; the threat of loss prevents withdrawal. When fear of divine punishment outweighs faith in divine love, obedience becomes self-protection instead of devotion.

This isn't new. Fear has been a reliable management tool, from ancient myths about angry gods to modern teachings about eternal judgment. It maintains order, but it rarely produces wisdom. A fearful believer may follow rules but rarely learns trust.

The Cycle of Dependence

These elements, authority, belonging, and fear, create a self-sustaining loop.

1. The leader offers certainty.
2. The group reinforces belonging.
3. Fear prevents exit.
4. Obedience maintains the system.

Everyone plays a role, even those who feel trapped by it. The system survives because it meets real human needs: safety, purpose, and connection. Breaking the cycle doesn't mean rejecting faith; it means maturing within it, moving from dependency to discernment.

Discernment as Liberation

Discernment is the inner compass that allows faith to evolve without losing its essence. It's the ability to listen to teaching while still thinking critically, to respect leadership without surrendering autonomy. True spiritual maturity invites dialogue, not silence. It encourages learning, not blind loyalty.

The healthiest communities are not those without structure, but those where structure remains transparent and accountable. In those spaces, leaders remain learners, giving remains voluntary, and questioning is seen as a sign of engagement, not rebellion.

Returning to Balance

Understanding the architecture of control allows us to rebuild architecture for empowerment. When people know how systems operate, they stop confusing control with care. They can honor the leadership role while recognizing their own authority within. That's the beginning of spiritual sovereignty, faith that functions with awareness.

Control thrives on ignorance. Freedom grows through understanding. The goal isn't to tear down religion but to design it consciously so that faith remains a relationship, not a regulation.

Chapter 3: The Psychology of Belief and Belonging

At the core of every belief system is a search for safety.
Faith offers answers where life offers uncertainty. It gives language to mystery and comfort to fear. When people find something that makes sense of their pain or gives purpose to their struggle, the bond runs deeper than logic. That bond is what makes belief so powerful and what makes it hard to question.

The Human Need for Meaning

Human beings are meaning-makers. We interpret events to survive them. We tell stories to explain what we can't control. At its healthiest, religion gives those stories structure and a framework to understand suffering, morality, and destiny. When done well, it becomes a source of peace. When misunderstood, it becomes a filter that limits growth.

The same exact mechanism that helps people trust in God can make them trust without discernment. Once belief offers stability, the mind resists any information that threatens it. Psychologists call this *cognitive dissonance* the discomfort of holding conflicting truths. Instead of confronting that discomfort, most people choose consistency. It feels safer to stay convinced than to feel confused.

Emotional Security and Spiritual Authority

Faith fulfills emotional needs long before it satisfies intellectual ones. People often come to religion seeking relief, healing, or identity. The rituals, songs, and sense of community activate feelings of safety that the brain associates with belonging. Over time, the emotional bond to the group becomes stronger than the original spiritual conviction.

This is why people remain even when teachings begin to feel restrictive. The body remembers safety, not theology. Leaving a religious community can feel like leaving family, culture, and purpose simultaneously. The pain of separation often outweighs the promise of freedom, at least at first.

The Power of Reinforcement

Belief thrives on reinforcement. Every answered prayer, every uplifting message, every moment of connection confirms that "this works." The human brain is wired to seek patterns; it notices what supports the existing narrative and ignores what challenges it. This selective attention strengthens conviction. What starts as faith becomes familiarity, and familiarity becomes truth.

Organizations understand this, often without realizing it. Regular meetings, testimonies, and communal celebrations create positive feedback loops. The energy of collective worship feels real because the human nervous system responds to unity. But without self-awareness, this same energy can disguise manipulation. People can mistake emotional charge for divine confirmation.

Trauma, Trust, and Dependency

Many who become deeply attached to religious systems have experienced trauma or instability before. Faith provides structure where chaos once lived. For a person recovering from pain, that structure feels like healing. In psychology, this is known as *trauma bonding,* forming strong attachments to systems or people who provide both comfort and control.

This doesn't mean believers are weak; it means they are human. Everyone seeks safety; religion has historically been the most accessible form of collective healing. The problem arises when comfort replaces curiosity. Once dependency sets in, growth slows, and questioning feels like betrayal.

The Role of Identity

Belief becomes identity when faith shifts from "what I believe" to "who I am." This transformation has both beauty and risk. When identity is rooted in faith, it provides deep purpose. However, independence feels dangerous when identity is rooted in belonging to a group. People begin to measure their worth by aligning with doctrine rather than with truth.

This is why disagreement feels like a personal attack and why many communities silence dissent it threatens the group's shared sense of self. Yet, true spiritual maturity allows identity to evolve without fear. Growth should not be seen as betrayal but as evidence of living faith.

Awakening and Awareness

Spiritual awakening rarely begins with new information. It begins when old explanations stop working. When people can no longer ignore contradictions, their minds open to reevaluation, and that process is uncomfortable but necessary. It dismantles dependency and reintroduces personal responsibility.

Awareness doesn't mean abandoning belief. It means understanding the *why* behind it. It's the shift from automatic faith to conscious faith, from needing answers to seeking understanding.

Returning to Conscious Connection

Recognizing the psychology behind belief doesn't make faith less sacred; it makes it more intentional. Understanding how belonging, fear, and reinforcement shape devotion helps believers participate with awareness instead of attachment. It restores balance between the heart and the mind.

Healthy faith invites both trust and thought. It allows people to experience God personally while still valuing community. Belonging then becomes partnership, not possession.

When people understand their psychology, they stop confusing emotion for evidence and control for care. They begin to practice faith as a dialogue, an ongoing exchange between self, Spirit, and truth. That is the foundation of spiritual maturity and the path back to freedom.

Chapter 4: The Economics of Faith: How Belief Becomes Currency

Faith has always had value. From the beginning, belief has been exchanged sometimes for comfort, sometimes for status, and often for survival. From the earliest rituals to livestream sermons, belief has functioned as both a spiritual and social exchange. What changed over time was *how* that exchange was measured and maintained. Over centuries, religion refined this exchange into a system combining devotion with economics, creating one of humanity's most enduring currencies: faith.

The Birth of Spiritual Exchange

In early civilizations, offerings were acts of gratitude and simple reciprocity. People gave what represented life to them: grain, fruit, livestock, to honor the unseen forces that sustained existence. The exchange was relational, not transactional. It symbolized trust between humanity and the Divine. No one expected a guaranteed return. The act itself was the blessing.

As societies grew, communities grew, organizations followed, and these offerings became structured. Temples needed caretakers, rituals needed organization, and priests needed resources. Out of practicality, worship became administrative, tracking who gave, when, and how much was the first framework of religious economy. The concept of *sacred contribution* emerged, which we now call tithes or donations. Over time, the purpose of giving shifted from participation to obligation. The more structured religion became, the more giving became a requirement for belonging.

From Gratitude to Guarantee

Eventually, the meaning of giving changed. Gratitude turned into spiritual insurance. People were taught that giving didn't just honor God; it *activated* God. The more you gave, the more blessed you would become. This belief *that transactions could influence divine favor* turned faith into an early form of commerce. The psychological weight of the exchange deepened. Instead of "I give because I'm thankful," the message became "I give so I'll be blessed." The offering was no longer just a symbol of faith; it became proof of faith. Giving began to represent spiritual standing, a visible measure of devotion.

This shift didn't happen out of greed but out of fear and need, but the shift marked a turning point. What began as community sharing evolved into an economic model. The temple or church became a spiritual center and a financial hub, funding social programs, supporting leaders, and maintaining property. At its best, this system provided stability. At its worst, it equated holiness with income.

The Financial Framework of Faith

Every organized religion eventually develops infrastructure, property, payroll, communication, and outreach. Those needs require funding, and funding requires participation. To meet those needs, leaders create systems that reward consistency and loyalty. Regular tithes, offerings, and service become the lifeblood of the institution.

The challenge arises when spiritual vitality begins to depend on financial stability. When giving declines, programs shrink; when programs shrink, leadership appeals to the congregation's fear of lack. The intention may be sincere, but the outcome is predictable: faith becomes a product to maintain rather than a relationship to nurture.

The Rise of Religious Industry

As faith spread through printing, broadcasting, and eventually the internet, religion adopted the same financial logic as business. Books, recordings, conferences, and branded merchandise made belief portable and profitable. Nonprofit status allowed ministries to operate with corporate efficiency while maintaining spiritual authority.

The term *prosperity gospel* captures this evolution clearly: faith framed as investment, blessing as return. Followers are taught that giving activates favor and that wealth validates righteousness. This message appeals to hope and human psychology.

The pattern isn't always malicious; it's systemic. When a movement depends on funding to exist, it must inspire people to give. Sermons become campaigns, testimonies become advertisements, and miracles become marketing. The emotional experience of worship blends seamlessly with the logic of sales.

The Psychology of Seed Faith

Financial giving in religious settings often uses the language of agriculture: sowing, reaping, and harvest. The metaphor is beautiful but easily manipulated. In ancient times, sowing was a cooperative act—trusting that nature and community would work together to produce abundance. In modern faith economics, that metaphor often carries conditional promises: *the more you sow, the more you grow.*

This equation works psychologically because it offers a sense of control over uncertainty. People want their lives to improve, and giving becomes a tangible action toward invisible outcomes. It's not greed; it's human nature, the desire to partner with something bigger in shaping destiny.

Nonprofit Doesn't Mean Profitless

Religious organizations operate as nonprofits in most nations, exempt from taxes and public scrutiny. This means they don't pay taxes and must reinvest revenue into their mission. The intent is to free spiritual work from political interference. The side effect is minimal financial transparency. Congregations rarely know how their contributions are used. For ethical leaders, this freedom is stewardship; for unaccountable ones, it becomes secrecy.

Nonprofit doesn't mean no income. Salaries, travel, media production, and building costs still require funding. The transparency gap appears when financial accountability becomes secondary to spiritual authority.

The absence of oversight doesn't always mean corruption; it often means tradition. Many systems have never been required to show the books. However, when the public begins questioning how faith handles finance, those who practice transparency become models of integrity rather than targets of suspicion. When leaders are treated as beyond question, financial oversight weakens. The trust is deep, but so is the risk. Without a balanced structure, even good intentions can become exploitation through neglect.

The Currency of Attention

In the digital age, money is no longer the only measure of devotion. Attention has become the new offering plate. Views, shares, and engagement are the modern tithe. Platforms reward virality, not virtue, so ministries and influencers alike adapt their message to stay visible. The more provocative the content, the higher the reach and the greater the revenue. A viral sermon can fund a ministry overnight. The danger is that messages start adapting to metrics. When engagement becomes the goal, truth becomes negotiable.

These dynamics turn spiritual truth into market content. Faith-based content now competes in the same marketplace as entertainment. Short clips replace sermons. Emotion outperforms depth. The economics of attention shape what people believe because visibility feels like validation. The sacred becomes branded, and popularity replaces principle as proof of calling. The economics of faith now depend as much on analytics as on anointing.

Stewardship Versus Salesmanship

Money itself is not the issue; money itself is neutral. It reveals motive. When used wisely, it sustains outreach, education, and community care. When misused, it distorts purpose. The difference lies in stewardship transparency and intention, whether giving is a partnership or performance. A healthy faith economy teaches that contribution is voluntary, not obligatory, and that abundance flows from alignment, not anxiety. It teaches the ability to manage resources without manipulating hearts.

Healthy spiritual economies invite transparency and teach financial literacy. They encourage people to give from choice, not pressure, and to view contribution as a partnership, not a purchase. In these spaces, generosity fuels growth without becoming a test of worthiness.

Restoring Balance

Understanding the economics of faith isn't about rejecting giving; it's about reestablishing alignment. Understanding how belief becomes currency helps believers return to conscious participation. It allows communities to honor tradition without becoming trapped by it. When done with awareness, giving reconnects people to gratitude rather than guilt. Resources are necessary, but they should never replace a relationship with God. Contribution is sacred when conscious and people give with awareness rather than obligation.

The business of religion doesn't need to disappear; it needs to evolve. When leaders embrace accountability and communities practice discernment, money returns to its rightful place as a tool, not a test.

Faith was never meant to be a transaction. It was meant to be a trust.

Chapter 5: The Marketplace of Modern Spirituality

Spirituality has always evolved with culture. Honestly, every generation reinvents how it connects with the Divine, finding new language, symbols, and tools. What used to happen through temples and pulpits now unfolds through timelines and platforms. In the past, that meant new denominations or reform movements. The internet has turned spirituality into an open market where anyone can publish a revelation, offer healing, or sell enlightenment in a few clicks. It didn't create new beliefs; it gave old ones a new stage.

The Age of Accessibility

For much of history, spiritual knowledge was guarded. Access came through hierarchy priests, pastors, scholars, or initiates. The digital era changed that. Anyone can study theology, astrology, psychology, or mysticism with one search. People who once felt excluded from religion now build personal practices drawn from multiple traditions.

This openness has helped millions rediscover their relationship with God on their own terms. It has also blurred the line between guidance and influence. A message can now reach millions instantly, without accountability or context. The same platform that spreads wisdom can also spread confusion.

The Digital Pulpit

Online platforms have replaced most physical barriers to entry. A ring light and Wi-Fi connection can reach more people than the largest sanctuary. What used to take years of study or ordination now takes visibility and confidence. In many ways, that democratization is progress, as wisdom once hidden inside institutions can now reach people who might never step into a church.

But accessibility comes with a price. When faith becomes content, the message must compete for attention. Algorithms reward emotion, not accuracy. The loudest voices rise fastest, and sincerity is often confused with expertise. The spiritual teacher, influencer, and entertainer now share the same stage, sometimes becoming indistinguishable.

Faith in the Attention Economy

Modern spirituality thrives in what economists call the attention economy. The most valuable resource isn't money, it's focus. Social media rewards emotion, relatability, and speed. Posts that inspire hope or provoke outrage travel fastest. As a result, teachers, coaches, and ministers often feel pressured to condense complex truths into bite-sized inspiration.

That doesn't make their messages false; it just limits depth. Spiritual truth rarely fits into 60 seconds, but the algorithm will show it in 60 seconds. Over time, spirituality adapts to the system. Emotional connection becomes the product, and attention becomes the offering.

Celebrity Conversions and Public Piety

Public spirituality has become a kind of performance art. In recent years, celebrity "coming-to-God" moments have filled timelines. Celebrities and influencers speak openly about faith, sometimes from genuine transformation, other times as part of a personal rebrand. Either way, faith has reentered popular conversation. That visibility helps normalize belief but also commodifies it. The pattern itself reveals how spiritual identity has become a branding tool. Posting scripture or sharing a testimony signals transformation and relatability. It builds trust with audiences who crave authenticity in a world saturated with performance.

This dynamic isn't about malice; it's about market behavior. The system rewards what people click, not necessarily what helps them grow. When faith becomes part of a brand strategy, belief merges with marketing. The message spreads, but so does confusion about what it means to live it. People start following personalities instead of principles.

The Rise of Spiritual Consumerism

Beyond religion, an entire spiritual marketplace has emerged, with courses, retreats, mentorships, and energy readings, all promising transformation. Many are valuable; others mirror the same patterns of dependency found in organized religion. The digital age turned belief into lifestyle. Apps deliver daily devotionals; subscriptions promise guided meditations, affirmations, and prophetic insights. Access costs, membership renewals, and "exclusive wisdom" replace pews and tithes with programs and price points. Spirituality is no longer confined to any religion; it's a marketplace of methods promising the same outcome: peace, purpose, abundance.

The problem isn't that people pay for learning or healing, it's when the exchange depends on emotional pressure or promised miracles. The soul cannot be sold, but it is often advertised that way in the modern market. This variety can be liberating for seekers. For those ungrounded, it can be disorienting. The abundance of options makes discernment essential. Many online "ministries" or coaching collectives operate like micro-churches or cults without formal doctrine, offering belonging, mentorship, and meaning for a price. The exchange is no longer donations for worship but payments for transformation.

Algorithms and Authority

The challenge for today's seeker is not finding information but filtering it. The internet doesn't curate truth; it curates' engagement. What spreads fastest becomes what feels real. This subtly shapes modern spirituality: teachers simplify complex truths to fit short clips, and nuance disappears in favor of clarity that converts.

Influence then becomes a new kind of ordination. The more followers someone has, their message is accepted as revelation. Without shared accountability, personal charisma replaces collective discernment. Communities form around individuals rather than ideas; when those individuals fail, entire movements collapse with them.

The Cost of Viral Faith

Healthy spirituality in the digital age requires slowing down. It asks us to listen beyond the performance to measure messages by fruit, not followers. A teacher's depth is not found in their reach but in the integrity behind their words.

Viral faith is fast but shallow. It ignites emotion but rarely roots understanding. Moments of conviction online can inspire genuine change, but they fade without structure to sustain them. A post can remind people of God, but cannot replace the lifelong process of knowing God.

For creators, the constant demand for content can turn devotion into performance, and the need to stay relevant pressures them to produce revelations on schedule. Inspiration becomes a job, and burnout follows. Many start with calling and end with exhaustion.

Toward a Conscious Marketplace

Technology itself is neutral; it amplifies whatever energy we bring. It promotes compassion, education, and empowerment across borders when used intentionally. When used with integrity, it connects teachers and learners, fosters compassion, and builds awareness across cultures. The key difference is in consciousness: whether the goal is service or sales.

Healthy digital spirituality values education over excitement. It invites people to learn rather than consume, to practice rather than perform. The future of faith will depend on how well we balance freedom of expression with the responsibility of influence.

Both teachers and seekers share responsibility in shaping that space. The teacher must remember that influence is stewardship, not ownership. The seeker must remember that guidance is a tool, not a substitute for inner wisdom.

Returning to Integrity

The marketplace of modern spirituality is a mirror. It isn't proof that faith has failed, it's evidence that humanity is still searching. The goal now is not to retreat from progress but to use awareness to navigate it. When people engage consciously, technology becomes a bridge rather than a barrier.

Authentic spirituality doesn't need a platform to validate it. Its power is in transformation, not transaction. Whether spoken in a temple or shared through a post, the truth remains: connection to God was never meant to be bought; it was meant to be lived.

Awareness allows believers and teachers to use platforms without losing purity to share truth without selling it.

Faith doesn't need to compete to stay relevant. It simply needs to remain real.

Chapter 6: The Industry of Influence - The Human Cost of Being Followed

Influence is a strange kind of power. It begins with the intention to help, share, and reach. But the more people listen, the more the message can change shape. Visibility magnifies everything: the purpose, the pressure, and the performance.

In faith and spirituality, influence once meant service. A teacher, prophet, or guide lived the message, often quietly, modeling devotion through humility and discipline. Today, influence has become measurable views, followers, engagement, applause. What used to be a calling now often feels like a career. A single post can crown someone a voice of truth before they've had time to live the message they speak.

The Weight of Being Seen

Being seen can feel like a blessing until it becomes a burden. Every word is watched, every silence questioned. The digital world made connections instant but also constant. The same accessibility that allows messages to spread worldwide also keeps leaders perpetually exposed. Every post, prayer, or word is open to judgment and interpretation. The need to maintain relevance can quietly replace the desire to remain authentic.

Even sincere leaders feel the tension between presence and performance, the expectation to always be "on," always confident, always inspiring. The same gift that connects them to others begins to pull them away from themselves. When every thought becomes content and every silence risks invisibility, making rest feels like negligence.

Validation and Vulnerability

Affirmation is powerful fuel. Validation is a natural human need, but under influence, it becomes amplified. Approval can feel like confirmation from God, and criticism can feel like spiritual warfare. Over time, leaders may begin to equate worth with reach and measure purpose by metrics.

The danger is subtle: attention becomes affirmation, and affirmation feels like truth. The line between devotion and dependence blurs again, this time not for the follower but for the one being followed. Validation turns into quiet captivity, not because people crave fame but because humans crave belonging, and being followed can feel like being loved.

Even the Light Needs Distance

Every sacred tradition includes the image of withdrawal. Moses left the camp to meet God on the mountain. Jesus retreated from the crowds to pray alone. Monks and mystics sought silence not to escape people, but to remember who they were without them.

They understood something the modern world forgets: the soul needs space to stay whole. Constant visibility fragments it. Even spiritual light requires distance to stay pure. Influence without solitude eventually distorts the soul.

The Performance of Purpose

When faith becomes a profession, performance follows. Messages are curated, tone adjusted, and moments of vulnerability edited for impact. None of this is inherently wrong; it's adaptation. But in the process, you lose the freedom not to know, grow privately, or learn without an audience.

The most visible leaders often carry invisible burdens, fatigue, loneliness, and pressure to remain inspiring even when they are exhausted. Influence feeds on consistency; humanity does not. The result is quiet erosion, where sincerity survives but joy fades as Influence without solitude eventually distorts the soul.

The Cost of Crowds

Influence magnifies the message and also the mirror. Leaders stop evolving because growth requires privacy, and privacy feels unsafe when every shift is public record. The crowd's gaze freezes them in the version people want to believe in. Followers project expectation, often confusing presence with perfection. The leader becomes a symbol more than a self. When the symbol fails to match the projection, faith not just in the leader but also in the message can fracture.

The crowd's love is powerful, but it is rarely patient. It can exalt and exhaust with equal speed. Even the most grounded voice risks becoming the product of people's hunger rather than a servant of their healing.

The Quiet Truth

The human cost of being followed is not always collapse; sometimes it's simply the slow loss of peace. The noise of admiration and critique drowns out the still voice that called the person to serve in the first place.

The real test of leadership isn't how many people follow you, but whether you can still hear yourself when they do. Influence amplifies both light and shadow. It's not evil, it's energy. Without self-awareness, that energy burns instead of builds. Authentic leadership was never meant to be performed; it was meant to be practiced. The strength of a message is not in how many people hear it, but in how deeply it remains lived by the one who carries it.

Influence can spread light or distort it, but the difference lies in distance. Knowing when to speak and when to step back is not retreat; it is remembrance. Even the brightest flame must guard its center to keep from burning out.

Chapter 7: Faith, Power, and the Politics of Control

Religion and politics have always shared the same language: faith, loyalty, and belief. Both promise protection, purpose, and belonging. Both reward obedience and punish dissent. The methods look different, but the psychology is nearly identical.

Faith has always shaped power, and power has always known how to use faith. From kingdoms to campaigns, belief has been the invisible hand guiding visible decisions. Religion offers moral legitimacy; politics offers protection and privilege. Together, they form a partnership that has ruled hearts and nations for centuries.

The Shared Architecture of Control

Religion and government are built on the same psychological framework: belief, obedience, and belonging. Both depend on loyalty to an unseen order, a moral law, or a social contract reinforced through repetition, ritual, and reward. One shapes the soul, the other shapes society, yet both rely on public trust. The line between faith and governance begins to blur when their interests align. Citizens are called *patriots* the same way followers are called *believers.* Each system promises safety in exchange for submission.

From royal decrees claiming "divine right" to modern political endorsements from pulpits, power has long known how to dress itself in scripture. When morality and law become indistinguishable, belief turns into infrastructure. Neither begins corrupt. Both arise from human need, the desire for order, justice, and meaning. But when one controls the other, the sacred becomes strategic. Faith starts to serve power instead of truth.

The Political Pulpit

In every era, the pulpit has influenced policy, sometimes toward justice or control. The pulpit has long been a political tool. In the United States, religious rhetoric helped justify independence, abolition, segregation, and civil rights, often on opposite sides of the same scripture. Political leaders learned early that if you want to move a nation, speak in the language of morality. The same verses that built division have also built deliverance. What changes is who's speaking and what they stand to gain.

Modern politics still borrows religious rhythm: the rally as revival, the speech as sermon, the promise as prophecy, good versus evil, salvation versus destruction, us versus them. Candidates present themselves as moral saviors; opponents become the embodiment of sin. Fear becomes the altar call, the faithful vote as the faithful worship not always from reason, but from belonging. Voters respond not just to logic, but to language that feels sacred.

The Price of Exemption

The U.S. tax system transformed this relationship into a quiet bargain. The tax-exempt status of churches under Section 501(c)(3) was meant to protect religion from political interference. But the protection comes with invisible strings. Under the Johnson Amendment, religious organizations can't publicly endorse or oppose political candidates without risking their exemption. In theory, it keeps pulpits neutral; in practice, it keeps them compliant. Preachers who question policy risk their exemption. Those who comply enjoy privilege. Over time, silence becomes a strategy.

Recent policy shifts have blurred those boundaries. Political administrations can quietly loosen or tighten enforcement, allowing some leaders more latitude than others. When a pastor's sermon can influence an election, neutrality becomes negotiation. Freedom of faith becomes conditional freedom protected only so long as it serves public order, and the freedom to preach becomes a form of managed speech with fine print.

Tax benefits often act as silent levers of control. They reward participation in a system while discouraging confrontation with it. When faith institutions rely on those benefits to survive, conviction can become caution. Silence turns into self-preservation.

The Economics of Division

Politics and religion both thrive on loyalty, and loyalty requires contrast. Every "us" needs a "them." Outrage raises ratings, donations, and engagement. Entire political strategies depend on moral polarization: if people believe their soul or nation is at stake, they'll fund the fight.

This is where lobbying meets the pulpit. Donors fund movements that echo their values, and in return, policies shift in their favor. What looks like conviction is sometimes a transaction. Money becomes a modern tithe not to God, but to ideology.

The danger isn't belief; it's blindness. When people stop questioning where money flows, influence replaces inspiration. Campaigns, causes, and coalitions learn to mimic revival music, slogans, emotion, and unity because revival sells.

Policy, Language, and Leverage

Power doesn't always silence through force; it often silences through funding. Grants, partnerships, and tax incentives can determine what can and cannot be said. Institutions that challenge dominant policy risk losing access. Language becomes regulated currency. In recent years, programs have lost support for refusing to align with new policy language. What began as "values-based funding" becomes value enforcement.

An example is the recent rollback of Diversity, Equity, and Inclusion programs under new federal directives. While some hailed it as cutting bureaucracy, others saw it as erasing space for marginalized voices. The reality is complex: DEI initiatives were imperfect, sometimes symbolic, sometimes misdirected, yet they represented the promise of representation. Their removal reflects how political will can redirect national morality with the stroke of a pen.

Under new directives, many programs were defunded or dissolved, not always because they failed, but because their language no longer matched national messaging. When funding can be withdrawn for using specific terms, public virtue becomes dependent on political favor. Faith-based and nonprofit organizations learn to self-edit, not out of conviction but survival. The same mechanism that once kept pulpits apolitical now keeps them strategically quiet.

The Currency of Loyalty

Politics and religion both depend on loyalty, and loyalty depends on opposition. Every "us" requires a "them." Outrage creates engagement; engagement creates funding. This is why campaigns, causes, and churches use similar emotional patterns: fear, hope, and belonging. They sell safety in uncertain times.

Lobbying is simply a belief that is turned into a business. Donors fund conviction the way parishioners fund vision. In both cases, money moves morality. When significant contributions secure influence, devotion becomes a transaction. It's not always corruption, it's conditioning.

The Psychology of Allegiance & Obedience

People don't follow because they're weak; they follow because faith feels safer than doubt. Whether it's a congregation or a country, certainty unites. Doubt divides. Power thrives on that instinct. It teaches that questioning is rebellion, that unity equals righteousness, and that the more sacred the cause, the less accountability it allows.

At its root, control isn't enforced by force but by meaning. People obey systems that give their lives purpose. Whether it's a nation, a church, or a cause, allegiance provides identity. This is why moral narratives are so powerful: they offer both clarity and comfort. To question the system feels like betraying the family.

Governments understand this. They manage behavior through law and loyalty, shaping the stories people believe about who they are and who the enemy is. Once belief becomes identity, reason no longer matters.

Conditional Freedom

Freedom of religion sounds absolute, but in practice it's conditional. It depends on laws, funding, and public tolerance. The same system that protects belief can also police it. Faith remains free only as long as it remains helpful to order.

This doesn't mean faith itself is corrupt—it means systems are human, and humans manage belief the same way they manage everything else: through control, reward, and regulation.

The Mirror of Power

Religion, politics, and economics aren't separate empires; they are reflections of the same human need to belong, to be right, to feel secure. The danger is not that they exist, but that we forget they are human constructions, not divine ones.

Power will always find a pulpit, and the pulpit will always seek power. The only safeguard is awareness, recognizing when conviction becomes compliant and when privilege replaces principle.

Faith, at its essence, doesn't need permission or policy. It needs practice. When belief requires regulation to survive, it stops being faith and starts being franchise.

Chapter 8: When Devotion Turns to Dependency

Faith begins with freedom and connection. It reminds us that we're not alone and that life has meaning beyond survival. For many, devotion is the first doorway to peace after chaos. It gives life meaning, organizes values, and grounds uncertainty in purpose. But over time, devotion can shift from relationship to reliance. The same practices that once built strength can start to shrink it when belief becomes the only language a person is allowed to speak. Following becomes safer than thinking, and belonging replaces becoming.

The Architecture of Attachment

Humans are wired for attachment. We seek stability in systems that promise certainty. Church, community, and cause all meet the need to know who we are and where we fit. In its healthiest form, devotion grounds us. Yet when that devotion demands sameness instead of growth, it begins to mirror emotional dependency.

What looks like loyalty can slowly become learned helplessness. Instead of developing a personal relationship with the Divine, people start outsourcing that relationship to leadership. The voice of guidance becomes external, institutional, and eventually unquestionable.

The Subtle Shift

Dependency rarely feels like bondage at first. It feels like safety. The prayers, community, and rhythm of ritual create a sense of belonging that the outside world rarely offers. People don't cling to systems because they're naïve; they stay because those systems once saved them.

But spiritual safety can quietly become emotional captivity. When self-worth depends on approval from leaders or the group, autonomy begins to erode. The voice of authority replaces the voice of conscience. The believer stops asking, *"What does God say to me?"* and starts asking, *"What will they think of me?"*

The Cycle of Hope and Fear

Every controlling system operates on the same emotional formula: promise, reward, fear, repentance, and renewal.

Hope offers purpose.
Fear keeps you loyal.
Guilt enforces behavior.
Relief feels like grace.

The pattern keeps people engaged and loyal. Moments of empowerment are followed by guilt for wanting more. Fear of losing favor leads to over-commitment, and exhaustion is framed as proof of devotion.

It isn't manipulation alone; it's conditioning. That rhythm becomes addictive. The nervous system learns to equate intensity with intimacy, pressure with purpose. When peace feels unfamiliar, people assume something's wrong because calm has never been safe. This is how codependency hides behind devotion. It feels spiritual when it's psychological.

Burnout in the Name of Belief

Many people don't lose faith; they lose energy. They confuse depletion with discipline. When "serving" means constant output time, money, and obedience, faith turns into performance. Religious burnout doesn't come from disbelief; it comes from overperformance. Members volunteer until they collapse, give until they're broke, or serve until resentment replaces joy. Leaders experience it, too, caught between divine calling and human expectation. The result is the same: emptiness that looks holy from the outside.

This isn't limited to religion. Exhaustion shows up in Movements, workplaces, and even relationships. They mirror the same cycle: loyalty is rewarded, questioning is punished, and sacrifice is romanticized. The structure is cultural, not just spiritual.

The Psychology of Dependence

Psychologists describe dependency as the moment when external approval replaces internal guidance. Faith systems reinforce this by framing obedience as virtue. Members learn to outsource conscience for clarity. It feels easier to follow than to discern.

Over time, this erodes self-trust. People stop recognizing the voice of intuition or Spirit within. They confuse guilt with conviction and compliance with holiness. Dependency is rarely chosen; it's trained.

Why People Stay

Leaving isn't easy, even when the truth is obvious. People stay because community is currency. The group provides purpose, identity, and belonging. To walk away can feel like dying socially. And for many, the fear of hell is replaced by the fear of loneliness.

Dependency doesn't always mean brainwashing; sometimes it's emotional survival. When people finally step out, they're not rebelling, they're recovering.

Grief in the Exit

Leaving a belief system doesn't mean losing faith but grieving identity. Detachment isn't betrayal, it's detox. The grief that follows isn't weakness; it's withdrawal from certainty. You lose rituals, language, and structure. Even your worldview goes quiet. Healing requires learning to listen inward again, to trust intuition over instruction.

Grief deserves compassion, not ridicule. It's a sign of growth, not rebellion. Every transformation carries the loss of certainty, belonging, and approval, but what returns is freedom, discernment, and peace. Therapists call this *deconstruction*, but spiritually, it's more like reintroduction, the return to your own soul after years of outsourcing it.

A Culture That Rewards Exhaustion

Our broader culture celebrates the same dysfunction: grind culture, hustle validation, "no days off." Society often reinforces spiritual dependency because it mirrors its values: productivity over peace, performance over authenticity. Religious exhaustion feels familiar in a culture addicted to constant output. Both celebrate sacrifice and overlook restoration. Religion didn't invent this addiction; it just sanctified it.

Healing begins when people recognize the pattern, not when they renounce the faith. Awareness doesn't destroy devotion; it refines it.

Faith Without Strings

Healthy devotion creates strength, not submission. It invites questions. It expands capacity instead of caging it. Genuine faith doesn't require exhaustion or blind obedience; it requires honesty, curiosity, and balance.

When devotion matures, it evolves into discernment. That's the shift from dependency to freedom from following God through a system to walking with God through your own spirit.

The lesson here isn't to abandon belief, it's to recognize when belief has started owning you.

Because the moment faith costs you yourself, it's no longer faith, it's servitude dressed as salvation.

True faith doesn't demand exhaustion or silence. It invites maturity, the ability to love what taught you while outgrowing what limits you. Dependency fades when connection becomes personal again, when prayer feels like conversation instead of compliance.

Freedom in faith isn't rebellion; it's return. The return to a God that doesn't require burnout or performance to prove belief. The return to a spirit that trusts without fear. The return to devotion without dependency.

Chapter 9: Cults Without Crosses

Not every cult wears a cross. Some wear hashtags, logos, or hashtags of "love and light." Others wear ambition, activism, or brand loyalty.

Cults didn't disappear.
They just rebranded.

What used to happen in church basements now happens in comment sections and conference rooms. The vocabulary changed, but the structure didn't. They moved from hidden compounds to open platforms, communes to comment sections, pulpits to podcasts. The symbols changed, but the structure stayed the same: authority, belonging, belief, and behavioral control. Humans haven't outgrown cults; we've digitized them.

The Modern Mirror

Today, control doesn't require religion. It only requires influence. Social movements, online tribes, wellness collectives, and even business "families" can mimic the patterns that once defined religious cults. Each offers belonging, identity, and a sense of purpose, and each carries the risk of emotional entrapment when loyalty outweighs logic.

The mechanisms are psychological, not theological:

- **A charismatic leader** becomes the brand.
- **Doctrine** turns into curated content.
- **Tithing** becomes monthly subscriptions or product sales.
- **Evangelism** looks like sharing links and recruiting followers.
- **Excommunication** becomes cancellation or shadow-banning.

The language is new; the manipulation is ancient. Cults have always been less about theology and more about psychology. They thrive wherever humans crave certainty, connection, and meaning. The 21st century just gave them better marketing.

Today's "cults" are built from content, not commandments. Fitness programs, political movements, lifestyle brands, and even entrepreneurial "families" all tap into the same emotional circuitry that once kept followers inside sanctuaries.

They promise transformation. They create identity. They reward loyalty.
And like any faith system, they protect their leaders from accountability by calling criticism "negativity."

The Digital Congregation

Online, influence is the new "anointing." Followers gather not under steeples but under usernames, worshiping at the altar of personality. The modern prophet has a ring light and a marketing team.

Algorithms amplify charisma faster than discernment can catch up. Once a message gains traction, it becomes a movement. Once a movement monetizes, it becomes a machine. And machines have one rule: feed the audience or lose it.

The result? Communities that started as safe spaces for healing or learning can evolve into echo chambers of performance. Dissent isn't debated; it's deleted. Loyalty isn't encouraged; it's required.

The Need to Belong

The rise of "tribe culture" reflects a deeper human hunger for connection in a fragmented world. Digital life gives us constant contact but little intimacy. In that vacuum, belonging becomes a transaction. People join movements and follow personalities because it feels safer than facing uncertainty alone.

Psychologically, this is attachment by design. Online communities replicate the same dopamine cycles as religion: affirmation, alignment, reward. The follower feels seen; the leader feels validated. Each sustains the other.

The Business of Belief

Modern cults are profitable because belief scales. Whether an MLM promises financial freedom, a "healing" brand sells enlightenment, or a political influencer sells outrage, all use the same conversion model: inspiration, identification, and investment.

The most effective movements turn personal transformation into product marketing. You're not just buying a course or a supplement; you're buying a belonging. When belief becomes brand, the line between empowerment and exploitation blurs.

MLMs, for instance, often frame sales as sisterhood. Leaders use the language of faith — "manifestation," "alignment," "abundance" — to disguise a pyramid of dependency. Members stay loyal not because the product works, but because leaving means losing identity.

The MLM Mindset

Multi-level marketing and influencer "teams" are the clearest secular mirror of old religious hierarchies.

- There's always a mentor who is someone "anointed" by success.
- There's always a doctrine that abundance will come if you work harder, think positively, or stay faithful to the method.
- There's always the monthly buy-in or recurring subscription.
  And there's always some doubt, rest, or independence.

Psychologically, it's brilliant. Spiritually, it's exhausting. People confuse personal empowerment with participation in a system that keeps them investing forever. "Freedom" becomes another form of dependence, wrapped in affirmations and hashtags.

The Wellness Gospel

Even wellness spaces can become temples of control. The language is softer energy, alignment, vibration, but the hierarchy is the same. Teachers become gurus. Vulnerability becomes marketing. Healing becomes performance.

When every purchase promises enlightenment, the line between spiritual guidance and spiritual sales blurs. The irony is painful: communities created to free people from dogma sometimes recreate it with better branding.

Digital Discipleship

Influencer culture operates on the same emotional chemistry. The algorithm rewards charisma, controversy, and confidence, the same traits that sustain cult leadership. Followers equate visibility with credibility. The more a person shares, the more divine they appear.

Over time, audiences turn into congregations. Parasocial relationships mimic spiritual mentorship: followers confess, seek advice, and adopt belief systems curated by strangers. The influencer becomes both preacher and product. Algorithms curate identity by confirming bias. The more you engage, the narrower your world becomes. Soon you're surrounded only by people who think like you, sound like you, vote like you, and worship your favorite truth.

When criticism arises, dissenters are labeled "negative energy" or "haters." Isolation begins again, not in remote compounds but in comment threads. That's not community, it's containment. And it works, because belonging still feels good even when it's built on illusion.

The Language of Light

New-age and wellness communities often carry the same hidden hierarchy. "Love and light" becomes a way to silence discomfort. "High vibration" replaces "holiness," yet still divides the pure from the impure. Healing becomes performance; vulnerability becomes branding.

These spaces rarely begin with manipulation. They begin with genuine healing yoga, therapy, and affirmation. However, once hierarchy forms, the structure repeats: unquestioned authority, emotional exclusivity, and financial dependency dressed as empowerment.

When Empowerment Becomes Exhaustion

The modern cult doesn't always control behavior; it controls bandwidth. Constant content, perpetual engagement, and community upkeep drain emotional energy like religious over-service did. People confuse burnout for purpose.

In this version, devotion looks like consistency. You must post, comment, buy, and attend. The cost isn't tithes, it's attention. When algorithms replace altars, worship becomes scrollable.

The Same Mind, Different Temple

From Jonestown to Instagram, from self-help seminars to online conspiracies, the formula is the same:

1. **Promise certainty in a chaotic world.**
2. **Offer belonging through shared identity.**
3. **Reward loyalty; punish dissent.**
4. **Convert emotion into currency.**

Control is never about content; it's about structure. Whether the leader quotes scripture, sells skincare, or promotes ideology doesn't matter; the pattern is psychological.

The Currency of Conviction

Belief has always been profitable. The only thing that changed is the platform. Emotional manipulation now comes with analytics. Attention is the new tithe. The more you give, the more the system grows. Whether it's a politician selling outrage or a guru selling transcendence, the formula stays consistent:

1. **Promise transformation.**
2. **Frame doubt as disloyalty.**
3. **Monetize emotion.**
4. **Repeat until burnout.**

This isn't evil; it's engineered. Control, at its core, is about managing energy. The old church did it through doctrine. The modern world does it through data.

Reclaiming Discernment

Understanding this isn't cynicism; it's protection. Awareness doesn't mean mistrusting every movement; it means noticing when passion becomes pressure. Healthy communities expand identity; unhealthy ones shrink it. Authentic leadership teaches people how to think, not what to believe.

Faith may have started the story of cult dynamics, but humanity keeps rewriting the sequel. Every generation creates its own digital, social, and ideological temples. The work now is to carry consciousness into each new form, remembering that the mind is always the first church to guard.

Seeing that pattern doesn't mean walking away from belief. It means walking toward the truth without a leash. Discernment is the new devotion. Awareness is the new faith. In a world where everyone preaches, the sacred act is simply listening to your soul again.

Chapter 10: God Without the Gatekeepers

Reclaiming Faith, Conscious Connection, and Healthy Leadership

At some point, we realize we inherited language, rituals, and expectations long before we meet the Presence behind them. For a time, that structure helps. It gives faith form, eventually the form hardens into a filter, and we start mistaking the reflection for the Source.

There comes a point when you realize you were never separated from God; you were just taught to ask permission to connect. Every structure you've outgrown, religion, hierarchy, ideology, was never the Source itself. It was a doorway. Some doorways led to light. Others led to walls.

The goal was never to stay in the doorway; the goal was to step through. This is where awakening begins, not in defiance but in clarity. God was never lost; access just got outsourced.

Beyond Permission

For centuries, people were told they needed a translator to reach the Divine priests, prophets, pastors, or programs. Each promised to make God more reachable, but most became gatekeepers instead. The message was always the same: *You can find God, but only through us.* That idea built entire economies of salvation.

The pattern is predictable: what starts as guidance turns into governance. Sacred leadership quietly becomes spiritual management. A business model of dependence has replaced the message of empowerment. But you can't sell what people already carry. The spark of God doesn't need distribution rights or middle management. Authentic spirituality doesn't depend on titles, tax exemptions, or platforms. The moment we remove the gatekeepers, a direct relationship, a dialogue between the soul and its Source remains.

You don't need an audience to be anointed. You just need awareness.

What Healthy Faith Looks Like

Healthy faith begins when you realize you can go straight to the Source, and no membership is required. It doesn't reject teachers; it repositions them. Leaders stop being middlemen and start being mirrors. Their purpose is not to speak *for* God but to remind you that God still speaks *to* you.

Authentic leadership has boundaries. It's transparent, accountable, and humble enough to point beyond itself. It doesn't trap people in service; it teaches them how to serve with self-awareness.

Healthy faith doesn't demand control; it cultivates character. It welcomes questioning instead of fearing it. It empowers individuality while honoring community. It values peace over performance, humility over hype.

True spiritual leadership doesn't seek worship; it builds wisdom. It doesn't compete for followers; it creates space for freedom. A healthy leader points you back to your own discernment, not their approval.

You'll know it's healthy when:

- You can disagree without being dismissed.

- Giving feels voluntary, not pressured.
- Transparency is expected, not avoided or as a performance.
- Rest is honored as much as service.
- Accountability flows both ways.
- Love feels steady, not conditional.
- Guidance feels like empowerment, not guilt.

When those traits exist, the structure supports growth instead of ownership.

From Religion to Relationship

Direct faith doesn't need ceremony to be sacred. It lives in awareness: a breath before reaction, gratitude between tasks, silence between prayers. God has never belonged to a denomination, a doctrine, or a brand. Every tradition holds fragments of truth; none contain the whole. The goal isn't to abandon worship, it's to understand why it works. Once you understand that, you stop defending institutions and start experiencing intimacy.

Prayer stops being performance; it becomes a conversation.
Worship stops being a ritual; it becomes

awareness.
Scripture stops being law; it becomes language.

When the connection is direct, faith becomes alive again. You begin to sense the same Divine energy in silence, in laughter, in the details of daily life. You begin to see that ritual is only powerful when it leads to a relationship. The candle, scripture, and song are all reminders, not requirements. They bring you back to the same truth: you and the Divine are not separate.

Healing the Fear of Freedom

Many people fear leaving systems because structure feels safer than stillness. But the silence that follows liberation isn't absence, it's invitation. What comes next is not isolation; it's intimacy. You start hearing your own spirit again.

Freedom doesn't make faith fragile; it makes it authentic. The God that survives your questions is the one worth trusting. When control falls away, integrity takes its place. Ethics return naturally because awareness replaces enforcement. You live by love, not fear. You practice accountability because you value connection, not because someone is watching.

That's what unmediated spirituality looks like: responsibility rooted in reverence.

The Return of Discernment

Spiritual maturity is the ability to hold truth without needing to control it. You can learn from anyone without surrendering your agency. You can respect leaders without making them idols. You can belong to a community without losing individuality.

That's what the gatekeepers were meant to teach but couldn't, because control is louder than trust. The antidote to control is consciousness. The more aware you become, the less manipulation can touch you.

Faith Without Fear

Fear-based religion keeps people dependent; love-based faith keeps them free.
You don't need threats of punishment to live with purpose. You don't need constant striving

to stay spiritual. God doesn't demand exhaustion as proof of belief.

Freedom doesn't weaken faith; it refines it. The strongest faith is one that can breathe, evolve, and still stand in love. Faith without gatekeepers doesn't end religion; it transforms it. Every gathering, every teacher, every text becomes a tool again, not a throne. The hierarchy dissolves into humanity.

The Quiet Reconnection

When you release the gatekeepers, the noise fades. The world stops feeling divided between sacred and secular. Every moment becomes spiritual. Every breath is communion.

You realize that the same energy once sought in temples or sermons has been speaking through intuition all along. You begin to see that sacred community was never meant to control belief; it was meant to remind us that we're not alone while we learn how to believe for ourselves. God without the gatekeepers is not a new religion. It's the oldest truth rediscovered.

The Divine lives in you, waits for your awareness, and answers without a middleman. God was never confined to the building; the building was just a mirror for what's inside you.

The work now is simple: keep that connection clean. Stay humble enough to learn, wise enough to discern, and brave enough to walk your path without a leash.

Because the truest expression of faith isn't obedience, it's **awareness**.

Chapter 11: Faith Ethics: Building Healthy Spiritual Systems

Awakening is only the beginning. Seeing the system is one thing, rebuilding it with awareness is another. Awareness means little without integrity. This is where responsibility begins. Once you understand how control, fear, and performance creep into faith, you can't unsee it. The next question is: *How do we create spaces that honor Spirit without repeating the same mistakes?*

Healthy faith systems are not born by rejecting structure but by reforming it, transforming hierarchy into harmony, power into partnership, and doctrine into dialogue. The goal isn't to destroy institutions; it's to redesign them with consciousness intact.

The Foundation of Integrity

The healthiest spiritual leadership is based on transparency, not mystique. Healthy spiritual systems are founded on integrity, not image. They don't depend on secrecy to maintain power. Secrets promote manipulation; honesty builds trust.

Transparency doesn't mean perfection; it means access. People should be able to see how decisions are made, where funds go, and who benefits. Integrity means the outside matches the inside. What's preached is practiced. What's promised is delivered. In communities where integrity leads, manipulation loses its power. When the pulpit becomes open-source, corruption has no air to breathe.

True leaders share power instead of hoarding it. They listen as much as they speak. They surround themselves with counsel, not followers. They see accountability as sacred, not threatening. People can handle human leaders; what breaks them is deception disguised as divinity.

Ethics as Energy Management

Every organization runs on energy, emotional, spiritual, and financial. When that energy circulates fairly, the community thrives. When it's siphoned upward through guilt, fear, or profit, it decays. Healthy giving feels open, voluntary, and informed. There are no hidden motives, no emotional sales pitches. Finances are discussed, documented, and shared because transparency builds peace.

Ethical systems treat giving as gratitude, not proof. They teach stewardship, not sacrifice. Offerings are transparent exchanges of support, not silent taxes on faith. The same principle applies to time and labor. Volunteers should feel appreciated, not obligated. Rest should be honored as devotion, not defiance. Balance is holiness in motion.

The Difference Between Service and Servitude

Leadership determines the spiritual climate in every generation. Unchecked ego corrupts ministries, movements, and collectives alike. The healthiest leaders understand that power isn't ownership, it's stewardship. Service flows from love. Servitude flows from control.

In healthy systems, participation is a partnership, and people are empowered to use their gifts freely. In unhealthy ones, service becomes performance, and exhaustion is treated as evidence of loyalty.

Leaders must consistently ask: *Are people serving from overflow or depletion?* The answer reveals the health of the system more than any sermon ever could. Leadership should amplify light, not absorb it. The true teacher points people back to their connection, not their approval.

Teaching Emotional Literacy

Spiritual maturity requires emotional maturity. Communities thrive when they integrate psychology into theology, when people understand how trauma, attachment, and identity shape belief. Modern spirituality must evolve beyond charisma into competence. You can't lead people spiritually if you can't understand them emotionally.

Trauma, projection, and codependency often shape how people connect to leaders and doctrine. When leaders lack emotional literacy, they mistake compliance for commitment and intensity for inspiration. Emotionally literate spaces teach members to recognize projection, codependency, and manipulation even when they come from the pulpit. This awareness doesn't weaken faith; it protects it. The soul and psyche are not competitors; they are collaborators.

Healthy ministries, wellness spaces, and collectives all need emotional intelligence training the same way they need financial ethics. Both are forms of spiritual hygiene. Emotional intelligence training should be as sacred as prayer. It teaches people to recognize manipulation, manage triggers, and discern Spirit from suggestion.

A spiritually literate community knows how to hold compassion *and* accountability simultaneously. Communities must normalize boundaries, rest, and autonomy. When members feel safe to say no, their yes regains meaning. When leaders rest, followers learn sustainability. Burnout isn't a badge of faith; it's a warning sign that energy has been misused.

Financial Integrity as Spiritual Practice

Money is energy, and energy reveals motive. When finances are transparent, trust multiplies. When they're hidden, faith erodes.

Practical steps are simple:

- Clear documentation of income and expenses.
- Independent audits or community oversight.
- Open discussions about giving, budgeting, and impact.

When people see where their energy goes, they give with joy instead of fear. Financial honesty is not a legal formality; it's an act of reverence and stewardship.

The Role of Education

Knowledge is the quiet shield that keeps faith from turning into fanaticism. Healthy communities teach context, historical, psychological, and practical. They don't hide from hard questions; they invite them. They treat learning as worship. Education is the bridge between devotion and discernment. A spiritually ethical organization doesn't just teach scripture or affirmation; it teaches critical thinking, history, and context.

Members who understand psychology, economics, and cultural evolution can recognize manipulation before it takes root. Ignorance breeds dependence; knowledge fosters independence and sovereignty. When people understand how belief works, they stop confusing emotion with evidence and become more resistant to manipulation. The new model of ministry should train thinkers, not just believers. Awareness and worship can coexist; in fact, they must. Faith should produce thinkers, not followers.

Building Communities That Breathe

A healthy spiritual system leaves room for individuality. It encourages people to evolve, question, and even leave without punishment. It celebrates growth, not conformity.

Healthy communities are ecosystems, not cages. People move in and out, learning and returning, and the structure remains stable because it's based on mutual respect, not control. Every organization, no matter how spiritual, needs checks and balances. Shared leadership models, open councils, and transparent communication prevent systems from centering around one ego.

The new standard of faith leadership is sustainability, not superiority. The question is no longer *"Who's in charge?"* but *"Is everyone flourishing?"* The future of faith isn't in mega-movements; it's in mindful communities, small circles that teach balance, spaces that heal without ownership, and leaders who see influence as responsibility, not entitlement.

Spiritual systems will still exist, but the new ones will breathe. They'll evolve, share knowledge, and allow movement in and out without shame.

The Future of Ethical Faith

When Ethics are involved, Leaders aren't celebrities; they're facilitators. Members aren't followers; they're co-creators. The collective energy circulates rather than funnels upward.

Faith becomes collaboration, not consumption. Success is measured not by attendance but by alignment and how people's lives feel when they leave the room. This is what modern spirituality must rediscover: partnership over performance, equality over hierarchy, humility over hype.

The next evolution of spirituality will be decentralized and based on conscious alignment. Circles instead of stages. Councils instead of celebrities. Collaboration instead of competition.

This doesn't erase leadership; it redefines it. The true measure of a leader will be how well they empower others to lead themselves. The church, the temple, the collective, the classroom — all can still exist, but with new DNA: clarity, consent, compassion, and community care.

The Evolution of Change

The age of blind obedience is ending. The era of conscious faith is beginning. This is the quiet revolution of faith: not another religion, but a restoration of responsibility. When ethics and empathy guide structure, faith becomes sustainable. When transparency replaces control, peace replaces fear.

Healthy systems don't fear accountability because they operate in alignment with what they teach. They embody love as structure, not a slogan. They make spirituality sustainable emotionally, financially, and energetically. Healthy systems don't need to convince you they're holy. You can feel it in the way they treat people. You can see it in how they handle truth. You can trust it because love is visible in the design.

If the earlier chapters dismantled illusion, this one plants the blueprint. Faith was never meant to be managed; it was meant to be *mirrored.* When leaders reflect love more than they demand it, when communities give freely instead of under pressure, and when Spirit moves without agenda, that's ethics in action.

That's God without gatekeepers becoming God with good governance.

That's the new ministry. That's the next era of faith. And it starts with leaders who remember: God doesn't need managers. God needs mirrors.

Chapter 12: The Return to Freedom

Freedom isn't the absence of faith; it's the purification of it.

You were never meant to live under someone else's version of God. Every ritual, every sermon, every rule was supposed to lead you inward, not bind you outward. Freedom is what faith was trying to give you all along. After the doctrines, deconstruction, and all the noise, authority, and performance, what remains is the quiet truth: You were always free. You were just taught to feel guilty for realizing it.

The return to freedom isn't about walking away from belief. It's about walking back to *yourself.*

The Journey Back to Center

You started this path seeking God. Somewhere along the way, you found systems. They gave you language, structure, and discipline until they demanded your soul's ownership. Most people don't lose faith; they lose the noise around it. They peel back the layers of fear, shame, and performance until Presence is all that remains.

You realize you never had to earn divine love; you just had to stop leasing it. The rules that once made you feel small were written by people trying to manage mystery. But God was never a manager. God was the mystery itself.

Awakening isn't about hating what helped you grow. It's about honoring the purpose it served and releasing what it no longer needs to control. The center of your faith was never the building, the leader, or the brand. It was the pulse behind every moment of clarity, peace, and truth. That's where freedom lives.

From Indoctrination to Insight

Healthy faith doesn't tell you what to think; it teaches you how to see. It invites you to explore, to study, to evolve. It doesn't demand allegiance; it inspires awareness. Indoctrination tells you what to think. Insight teaches you how to listen.

Authentic spirituality doesn't silence thought; it expands it. It asks better questions, welcomes paradox, and replaces fear with wonder.

Insight doesn't break belief; it refines it. Insight isn't rebellious, it's responsible. It means owning your relationship with the Divine instead of outsourcing it. It means evolving from student to steward.

You stop repeating memorized prayers and start living conscious ones.

Reclaiming the Mind and Soul

The mind was never the enemy of faith; it's the interpreter of it. When the brain and spirit work together, belief becomes intelligent love. You don't have to believe the same way forever. Faith is supposed to evolve; that's how truth stays alive.

Healthy faith allows logic to question, express emotions, and guide intuition. It recognizes that spirituality without thought becomes superstition, and intellect without spirit becomes arrogance. The two are partners, not rivals. You can outgrow theology and still love God. You can shift practices and still be sacred. You can lose certainty and keep a connection.

This is how spiritual maturity grows, not by surrendering the mind but refining it. Growth doesn't cancel what came before; it clarifies it.

The God that once felt confined to a pulpit now meets you in ordinary moments, the sunrise, the silence, the laughter that breaks tension.

The Freedom to Evolve

You can believe differently today than you did yesterday and still be faithful. That's the beauty of evolution, truth is alive.

Faith matures like people do through experience, humility, and curiosity. The moment belief becomes static, it becomes control. Freedom keeps faith dynamic, adaptable, and honest.

Evolving spiritually isn't betrayal; it's growth. Even the universe expands. Why shouldn't you?

The Sacredness of Self-Sovereignty

Self-sovereignty doesn't mean isolation; it means alignment. It means knowing that your intuition is sacred, your voice is valid, and your relationship with the Divine is yours to cultivate. Your soul isn't a franchise, it's a frequency. You're responsible for how you tune it.

The spiritual gatekeepers taught dependency because dependency pays. But when you realize you can hear God, you start to understand you can still learn from others without losing your authority. The most significant lie control ever told was that holiness required supervision. But no one can mediate your access to God. The same Presence that guided prophets and mystics still speaks through conscience, creativity, and peace.

Freedom means trusting the voice within that God gave you again.

Faith That Breathes

When faith is free, it breathes differently; it's alive. You stop performing and start participating. You stop chasing perfection and start choosing presence. There's no panic in missing a service, no shame in having questions, and no fear in learning from another path. Healthy faith feels like breath expanding, contracting, and moving. It's not something you schedule; it's something you live. It invites peace instead of pressure and purpose instead of punishment.

The rules dissolve into rhythm: gratitude, honesty, compassion, rest. These become your new commandments. Faith stops being a script and starts being a lived conversation between your humanity and your divinity.

That's the point of everything this book has explored: not to tear down belief, but to return it to its natural state, organic, evolving, alive.

The New Spiritual Landscape

The future of faith won't be about domination or doctrine. It will be about integration, merging spirit with science, psychology with sacredness, and community with consciousness.

This generation is learning to embrace truth and transparency, reverence and reason. We're not losing religion; we're refining relationships.

Healthy systems will survive, not because they control people, but because they care for them. Leadership will mature into mentorship. Worship will evolve into wisdom.

Freedom doesn't destroy faith; it redeems it.

The Final Return

In the end, awakening doesn't lead you away from God. It leads you closer without the noise, without the guilt, without the gatekeepers. You don't return to God by retracing your steps; you return by remembering who you were before someone told you how to be holy.

You realize God was never the sermon or the system. God was the silence between them. The freedom you've been chasing isn't rebellion; it's remembrance.

Because faith was never meant to be owned, it was meant to be *embodied.* And when it's embodied, you don't need permission to be whole. You just are. The real sanctuary was never a place. It was the awareness that you and the Divine were never apart.

Closing Reflection:
Faith is not for sale; God is not a business. The sacred belongs to everyone willing to listen. The temple has no doors now, only mirrors. And if you look closely, you'll see the same light that built the stars lives quietly inside you.

When Belief Becomes Binding: A Look at Modern Cult-Like Religions

Faith at its best frees the mind; at its worst, it cages it.
Every era has produced movements that began with good intentions, community, order, and purpose, only to transform into systems of control.

This isn't about labeling individuals or condemning all institutions; it's about **recognizing patterns that trade freedom for belonging.**

Across the landscape of modern religion and spirituality, several systems reveal how easily devotion can morph into domination.

Scientology

Scientology, born in the mid-20th century from L. Ron Hubbard's writings, is a path to spiritual clarity and personal empowerment. Yet its inner framework mirrors corporate hierarchy and military discipline, with confidential teachings, pay-to-progress levels, and an obsession with control.

Followers are promised enlightenment through structured "auditing," but access requires escalating financial commitments. Dissenters often face isolation, surveillance, and reputational shaming.
What began as a quest for personal evolution became an empire of compliance.

Core pattern: Knowledge and belonging are monetized; transparency is withheld until loyalty and payment are proven.

Mormonism (The Church of Jesus Christ of Latter-day Saints)

The Latter-day Saint movement began as a spiritual restoration, with powerful community values and a drive for family cohesion. Yet within some sectors of Mormonism, particularly its fundamentalist branches, the demand for obedience has overshadowed personal autonomy.

From polygamist offshoots to rigid social expectations around gender, purity, and authority, the culture can create spiritual performance pressure.
While many members live faithfully without coercion, others describe psychological conditioning rooted in guilt and conformity.

Core pattern: Structure and salvation intertwined so tightly that questioning becomes rebellion, not reflection.

Jehovah's Witnesses

This movement emphasizes purity, separation from the world, and loyalty to its governing body. For many, the sense of purpose and community is deeply fulfilling, but it can come at the cost of free will.

Strict information control, discouragement from higher education, and "disfellowshipping" (excommunication) create a cycle of fear that keeps members in line. Family and social ties are often severed for those who leave, turning belief into emotional blackmail.

Core pattern: Obedience sustained by fear of isolation; loyalty measured by silence, not understanding.

New Age Collectives and Modern "Spiritual Business"

Not all control wears a collar or quotes scripture. In recent years, "healing" communities, influencer-led programs, and manifestation networks have begun replicating the same cultic traits, only now wrapped in pastel branding and hashtags.

Followers are promised ascension, success, or divine favor through courses, memberships, or energy work. Leaders proclaim enlightenment while monetizing dependence. Once again, charisma replaces accountability, and "alignment" becomes a marketing plan.

Core pattern: Spiritual language weaponized for profit; enlightenment replaced by enrollment.

The Common Thread

Despite their differences, these systems exploit the psychological needs of belonging, purpose, and certainty.

Cults, churches, and collectives all thrive on one unspoken contract:

"We will give you meaning, if you give us yourself."

But true faith does not demand your autonomy. Healthy spirituality invites critical thought, community without coercion, and leadership that empowers rather than consumes.

When belief requires surrendering conscience, community demands compliance, and questioning equals betrayal, that's not devotion. That's **possession dressed as purpose.**

Closing Reflection

You don't have to renounce faith to reclaim freedom.
Recognizing manipulation doesn't make you cynical; it makes you conscious. Whether the doctrine is ancient or modern, branded or biblical, every soul has the right to choose connection over captivity.

Faith that frees you honors God.
Faith that owns you replaces God.

The Journey That Changed Everything

This book began with a single question that refused to leave me:
How could one body of believers be so divided?

That question sent me on a search across years, degrees, and disciplines. I studied psychology, theology, and human behavior. I read over 150 books, the Bible in seven different versions, and countless works on culture, science, and spirituality. Each one peeled back another layer of illusion until I began to see how belief systems shape minds, and how minds sustain systems — for better or worse.

At first, I wanted answers about religion. What I found was the architecture of humanity — the ways people build meaning, organize morality, and protect belonging. The deeper I went, the clearer it became that faith was never the problem. The business of managing faith was.

This realization didn't destroy my spirituality; it refined it.
It reintroduced me to God, not the one filtered through pulpits or politics but the living Presence that speaks through intuition, peace, and awareness.

Every psychology text, scripture, and sleepless night reading and questioning led me to the intersection of mind, soul, and freedom.

My hope is that this work doesn't just give you information; I hope it permits you to think, question, evolve, and rediscover the sacred for yourself. Once you start seeing the design of belief, you stop mistaking the walls for the wonder. And once you meet God without the gatekeepers, you never forget how direct that connection feels.

Thank you for walking this path with me.
May your search bring you back home to peace, power, and Presence.

Parting Note from the Author

If you made it this far, you've done more than read a book — you've reclaimed a piece of yourself.

I wrote this because I've lived both sides of belief — the devotion and the disillusionment, the worship and the wake-up. I learned that faith, at its best, doesn't need control to survive. It thrives in clarity, honesty, and freedom.

This isn't a call to abandon community. It's an invitation to build it better — with transparency, compassion, and consciousness. To gather because you want to grow, not because you're afraid to leave.

If this book resonated with you, let it be a mirror, not a monument. Keep asking, healing, and building systems that honor spirit and sanity. You don't need permission to walk with God.

You need awareness. And awareness, once found, can't be unlearned.

Welcome back to freedom.

— Dr. Kaci

Tools for Continued Reflection

(These sections are optional, meant to guide study, dialogue, and integration.)

Summary Charts: The Psychology of Belief

Dynamic	Religious Expression	Psychological Mechanism	Healthy Counterbalance
Authority	"Anointed" leader	Transference / projection	Shared leadership, transparency
Ritual	Structured worship	Behavioral conditioning	Mindful participation
Fear	Punishment / loss of favor	Trauma reinforcement	Education, reassurance, truth-based teaching
Guilt	Moral control	Internalized shame	Self-compassion, boundaries
Belonging	Group identity	Attachment security	Inclusion without conformity

Key Historical References

- Early religious institutions were instruments of governance and social order.
- The evolution of tithing from an agricultural exchange to a financial system.

- Influence of mass media and technology on modern spiritual movements.
- Parallels between political propaganda and religious indoctrination.
- Shifts in U.S. tax policy and the role of 501(c)(3) status in shaping speech.

(Encourage readers to trace how faith, finance, and power evolved together rather than separately.)

Questions for Reflection and Group Discussion

1. Where did your earliest understanding of God come from — and has it changed?
2. Which part of your faith experience felt empowering, and which parts felt controlling?
3. How do you discern between guidance and manipulation in spiritual settings?
4. What does "freedom in faith" personally mean to you?
5. What would it look like if you were to design a healthy spiritual community?

Suggested Reading and Continued Study

Psychology & Spiritual Behavior

- *The Power of Habit* — Charles Duhigg
- *The Road Less Traveled* — M. Scott Peck
- *Man's Search for Meaning* — Viktor Frankl

Religion & Society

- *The History of God* — Karen Armstrong
- *The Age of Reason* — Thomas Paine
- *The End of Faith* — Sam Harris

Awakening & Consciousness

- *The Untethered Soul* — Michael A. Singer
- *A New Earth* — Eckhart Tolle
- *Anatomy of the Spirit* — Caroline Myss

(Readers can add the works that shaped their awakening because continued learning keeps faith alive.)

Faith doesn't end with awareness. It begins there.
Awareness turns belief into wisdom, devotion into discernment, and worship into daily life.
Carry what you've learned into every space you touch — not as a weapon against the past, but as a light for what's possible next.

Familiar Cult Mechanics Across Belief Systems

(For Reflection, Education, and Awareness)

Cult Mechanic	Definition / Manifestation	Seen In	Psychological Effect
Information Control	Restricting or filtering what members read, watch, or hear. Framing outside sources as dangerous or "worldly."	Jehovah's Witnesses, Scientology, Fundamentalist movements, New Age influencer networks	Limits critical thinking; creates dependence on the group for "truth."
Isolation	Separating members from family, friends, or society that might challenge doctrine.	Jehovah's Witnesses, Polygamist sects, closed intentional communities	Increases emotional dependency and fear of rejection.
Charismatic Authority	Centralized, unquestionable leadership often viewed as divinely chosen or spiritually superior.	Scientology (Hubbard lineage), FLDS, Mega-ministry figures, "Gurus" in self-help cultures	Promotes obedience through awe or guilt; suppresses personal discernment.
Fear & Guilt Conditioning	Instilling fear of punishment,	Jehovah's Witnesses,	Creates internalized

Cult Mechanic	Definition / Manifestation	Seen In	Psychological Effect
	divine wrath, or failure if one questions or leaves.	Fundamentalist Christianity, prosperity theology, MLM-style "spiritual" programs	shame; replaces love-based faith with anxiety-based loyalty.
Financial Manipulation	Requiring payments, donations, or purchases for access to blessings, teachings, or status.	Scientology auditing levels, prosperity gospel churches, manifestation programs	Reinforces control through debt and guilt; equates money with worthiness.
Us vs. Them Mentality	Dividing believers from outsiders; branding dissenters as lost, unworthy, or evil.	All major high-control groups (religious or secular)	Reinforces conformity; discourages open dialogue.
Doctrine Over Personhood	Placing organizational rules above individual needs, mental health, or autonomy.	Strict sects, authoritarian ministries, hierarchical spiritual orders	Devalues self-trust; prioritizes obedience over well-being.
Language & Thought Control	Redefining common terms (sin, faith,	New Age movements, prosperity	Narrows perception; normalizes

Cult Mechanic	Definition / Manifestation	Seen In	Psychological Effect
	freedom, consciousness) to enforce conformity.	doctrines, high-demand faith systems	cognitive dissonance.
Exclusivity Claims	"We alone have the truth / path / revelation."	Scientology, certain Christian or New Age sects	Creates dependency; fosters spiritual elitism.
Reward & Punishment Cycles	Love-bombing newcomers, then withdrawing support when compliance fades.	Cultic churches, self-help groups, coaching collectives	Conditions behavior through emotional manipulation.
Secrecy & Hierarchical Access	Withholding "higher truths" until members prove loyalty, pay dues, or ascend ranks.	Scientology, esoteric sects, exclusive online teachings	Keeps followers striving and self-blaming for lack of progress.
End-Time or Apocalypse Narratives	Framing the world as doomed to instill urgency and obedience.	Jehovah's Witnesses, Fundamentalist sects, online conspiracy cults	Generates chronic anxiety; discourages long-term independent goals.
Exploitation of Idealism	Using members' desire to serve or	Church volunteers,	Creates burnout and

Cult Mechanic	Definition / Manifestation	Seen In	Psychological Effect
	heal others as unpaid labor or emotional currency.	"lightworkers," or inner-circle apprenticeships	disillusionment masked as devotion.
Suppression of Critical Dialogue	Silencing questions with scripture, shame, or spiritual bypassing.	Across both traditional and New Age groups	Prevents truth-testing and emotional growth.

💬 **Interpretation Notes**

Cults, churches, and collectives rarely identify as such. Control hides behind **language of love, purpose, or enlightenment.**
The goal is not to condemn belief, but to **illuminate behavioral patterns** that replace connection with compliance.

Healthy systems:

- Welcome questions without punishment.
- Encourage transparency and education.
- Allow members to grow, leave, and return without fear.

True faith is not afraid of scrutiny, only control is.

"Every system can start sincerely and end in manipulation if power goes unchecked.
Spiritual maturity begins when you can tell the difference between guidance and governance."

Thank you for your purchase. You can also follow us online on IG and FanBase @SpeakingFreedom, You can find our YouTube Channel yourtube.com/@speakingfreedomTV

Please check out our other books.

Faith 101

Faith 201

Faith 301

Faith 401

The Unknown Power

Spiritual Human

Behavior It's My Time

Beyond The Veil

No Religion, Just God

Messengers Among Us

Balance From Within

Understanding Immunity

www.ingramcontent.com/pod-product-compliance
Lightning Source LLC
Chambersburg PA
CBHW070115080526
44586CB00013B/1298